BEETHOVEN
by Berlioz

Ludwig van Beethoven

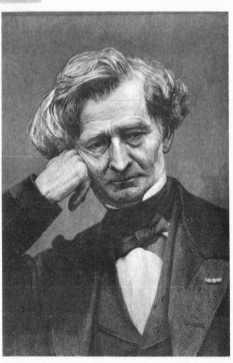

Hector Berlioz

Beethoven by Berlioz

a critical appreciation of Beethoven's
nine symphonies and his only opera —
Fidelio — with its four overtures

compiled and translated
by Ralph De Sola

CRESCENDO PUBLISHING COMPANY
BOSTON

Dedication and Gratitude

Dedication and gratitude are owing to attentive audiences, certain authors, and perceptive critics who seem to have joined forces in stimulating better and better performances of the works of at least two of the three great Bs of music: Bach, Beethoven, and Berlioz.

Most of us who read this book have participated as members of some audience or other. Certain authors such as Jacques Barzun, Sir George Grove, Ernest Newman, and Romain Rolland have revealed the transcendent modernism of Beethoven and Berlioz, illuminating the romantic era when Berlioz traversed the realm of melody in his collection of musical essays—*A travers chants*.

The greatest gratitude, however, is reserved for the many inspired instrumental and vocal performers of Beethoven and Berlioz. Conductors whose direction of the works of both composers was memorable include Sir John Barbirolli, Sir Thomas Beecham, Leonard Bernstein, Sir Adrian Boult, Herbert von Karajan, Otto Klemperer, Pierre Monteux, Charles Munch, Fritz Reiner, Arturo Toscanini, and your unmentioned favorites.

Beethoven experts certainly include Ansermet, van Beinum, Bernstein, Böhm, Boult, Casals, Walter Damrosch, Fürtwängler, Haitink, Eugen Jochum, von Karajan, Klemperer, Knappertsbusch, Kondrashin, Konwitschny, Leinsdorf, Zubin Mehta, Mengelberg, Monteux, Munch, Ormandy, Paray, Reiner, Solti, Steinberg, Stokowski, Szell, Toscanini, and Weingartner. And you are free to think of others who at first hearing brought about total integration between you and the music.

Berlioz specialists abound today as never before; but some of the best during the past half century include Beecham, Bernstein, Boulez, Boult, Cluytens, Colin Davis, von Karajan, Klemperer, Koussevitsky, Martinon, Mitropoulos, Monteux, Munch, Paray, Reiner, Rozhdestvensky, Sharples, Toscanini, and Roger Wagner.

My wife, Dorothy Clair De Sola, deserves credit for her sustained help during all stages of translation, compilation, and production. But all readers may owe the most to Mr. Phil Polito of San Diego who year after year supplied me with books, clippings, and records covering the entire field of great music, including the best of Beethoven and Berlioz.

January 1975   RALPH DE SOLA

Contents

Preface

Beethoven's Nine Symphonies, Fidelio — his only opera, and its over-tures, critical essays extracted from a book by Hector Berlioz: *A travers chants — études musicales, adorations, boutades, et critiques —* Traversing the Realm of Melody — musical studies, admirations, whims, and criti-cisms — was first published in Paris in 1862 by Michel Lévy.

The original book opens with Berlioz' report regarding the first per-formances of Beethoven's works in France where they were played incom-pletely and very poorly by the musicians of the Paris Conservatoire con-ducted by François Habeneck. Despite Habeneck's profound admiration of Beethoven's works he was unable to infuse the local musicians, and often played the symphonies with many cuts, or with movements of more popular symphonies interspersed, in an attempt to make them more attrac-tive to hostile hearers.

Berlioz' critical appreciation of Beethoven's nine symphonies follows. It is succeeded by a few paragraphs concerning Beethoven's religious music, and by a long chapter describing *Fidelio,* his only opera, and its four over-tures. The best of Berlioz' essays concern the nine symphonies and *Fidelio.* They are contained in this compilation and new translation.

The original book concludes with a short chapter about Beethoven's chamber music, his concertos, a Liszt performance of the third piano con-certo, plus a rather full account concerning the dedication of the Beethoven monument in Bonn, his birthplace, some eighteen years after his death. Berlioz tells how the boys of Bonn played on the street surrounding the new statue. They appeared utterly indifferent to the monument and to the figure of the great composer it honored.

The first account of the Beethoven celebration in Bonn appeared in the columns of a Parisian publication — *Journal des Débats.* Its pages carried many other accounts written by Berlioz, who was as accomplished as a critic as he was as a composer or as a conductor.

Berlioz listed many dignitaries and musical personalities who at-tended the Beethoven celebration held in Bonn (now capital of West Ger-many) on August 10, 1845. Berlin sent Meyerbeer and Jenny Lind — the Swedish Nightingale — who had been singing there; Vienna was repre-sented by deputies from its music conservatory, and by Prince Frederick of Austria; Salzburg by the director of the Mozarteum; Stuttgart by Lind-painter — its leading composer-conductor whose symphonies graced the first programs of the New York Philharmonic; Schindler, one of Beetho-ven's oldest friends, came from Aix-la-Chapelle (Aachen); Sax of saxo-phone fame came from Paris; Pleyel — the composer also famed for his success as a pianoforte maker — attended with his son and his daughter-in-law, a popular concert singer of the time; the Pleyels represented Brussels together with Fétis, its leading music critic; Saint Petersburg sent the editor of its leading newspaper; London, together with the ardent music-loving audiences of the British Isles, was represented by members of its Philharmonic Society, by its composer-conductors Ignaz Moscheles and Sir George Smart, as well as by Queen Victoria, who had taken vocal lessons from Mendelssohn, and was accompanied to Bonn by her consort, Prince Albert.

Berlioz also listed the wives of prominent composers and other musicians who came to the celebration, organized by Liszt and Spohr, although their husbands, for one overpowering reason or another, could not or would not attend: Spontini, Auber, Halévy, Thomas, Habeneck, Benedict, Mendelssohn, Marschner, Schumann, Glinka, and many others.

A brief chronology, prepared by the compiler of these essays by Berlioz about Beethoven, should aid readers trying to reconstruct something of the Romantic Era spanning the American and French revolutions, the Napoleonic wars, and the troubled period preceding the Franco-Prussian conflicts.

Ludwig van Beethoven born in Bonn (on the Rhine 16 miles below Cologne), December 16, 1770, year of the Boston Massacre.

First Symphony begun 1799. United States and France fighting undeclared naval war.

Second Symphony completed 1802.

Fidelio, opera, begun 1803, completed 1805, revised 1806 and 1814; first performed in Vienna in 1805 when city was occupied by Napoleon and his troops.

Third Symphony, *Eroica,* completed 1803, first performed 1805.

Fourth Symphony completed 1806.

Fifth Symphony begun 1805, completed 1807 — opening theme • • • ━ used during World War II as V-for-victory slogan encouraging under-ground forces hostile to the fascists and the Nazis.

Sixth Symphony, *Pastoral,* begun 1807, completed 1808.

Seventh and Eighth Symphonies completed 1812. Napoleon's retreat from Moscow.

Ninth or Choral Symphony, *Ode to Joy,* begun 1817, completed 1823.

Beethoven died in Vienna, March 26, 1827. The same year slavery was abolished in New York State.

Hector Berlioz born in La Côte-Saint-André (Isère — southeastern France), December 11, 1803. That year Robert Fulton was demonstrating a steamboat on the Seine.

Symphonie fantastique completed 1830. Year of the revolution replacing Charles X with Louis Philippe I.

Harold in Italy, combination viola concerto and symphony, completed 1834.

10

Requiem, mass for victims of the 1830 revolution, completed 1837.
Benvenuto Cellini, opera, completed 1838.
Romeo and Juliet, opera, completed 1839.
Treatise on Orchestration published 1843.
Damnation of Faust, opera, completed 1846. Year of the Mexican War.
Les Troyens, opera, completed 1859.
A travers chants: material used in this book collected between 1828, when Berlioz first heard Beethoven's symphonies performed in Paris, to 1862 when the book was first published during the American Civil War.
Berlioz died in Paris, March 8, 1869. The same year the financial Black Friday (September 24, 1869) occurred in the New York stock exchange due to gold cornering; also that year tracks of transcontinental railroad were completed, linking Atlantic and Pacific coasts of the United States.

11

SYMPHONY NO. 1   C major   opus 21

first movement: *Adagio molto; Allegro con brio*
second movement: *Andante cantabile con moto*
third movement: *Menuetto: Allegro molto e vivace*
fourth movement: *Finale: Adagio; Allegro molto e vivace*

This work, by its form, its melodic style, its sobriety of harmony, and its instrumentation, is altogether distinct from Beethoven's succeeding compositions. It seems evident the composer wrote it under the influence of Mozart whose ideas he sometimes enlarges, and everywhere imitates with ingenuity. Only in the first and second movements, however, one observes here and there, some of the rhythms used by the author of *Don Giovanni;* this is clear even if it occurs rarely and somewhat inconspicuously.

The first movement — Allegro — has a six-bar phrase as its theme; and although it contains nothing very characteristic, it is most interesting from the outset because of the exquisite artistry with which it is treated. This phrase is followed by an episodic melody in a style somewhat undistinguished; in the middle of a half cadence, repeated three or four times, we arrive at a woodwind passage imitating a quartette; to one's astonishment this already has been found in various overtures of French operas.

The Andante contains a kettledrum accompaniment, marked *piano;* today it seems quite common; but one can recognize it as the prelude to the startling effects he produced later on with these instruments used so little and so poorly by his predecessors. This movement, full of charm, presents a gracious theme; and it lends itself well to a fugal development the composer evolves ingeniously and piquantly.

The Scherzo (marked *Menuetto* in the score) is the first born of that family of charmingly humorous pieces in this form invented by Beethoven. He substituted the scherzo in nearly all his instrumental works for the minuet of Mozart and Haydn; the minuet's speed was but half; its character

13

was altogether different. This scherzo has exquisite freshness, agility, and grace. But neither here, nor in the rest of the symphony, is there anything one can qualify as truly new, musically speaking. It is the only real novelty in this symphony wherein poetic novelty is completely absent, notwithstanding poetic novelty being so grand and so rich in the greater part of his following works.

Certainly it is music admirably framed: clear, vivacious, although only slightly accentuated; cold, and sometimes even mean — as in the final rondo — truly musical childishness; in a word: Beethoven is not here. Let us find him.

SYMPHONY NO. 2   D major   opus 36

first movement: *Adagio molto; Allegro con brio*
second movement: *Larghetto*
third movement: *Scherzo; Allegro*
fourth movement: *Allegro molto*

In the D-major symphony, Beethoven's second, all is noble, energetic, stately, and audacious; the introduction (marked *largo*) is a masterpiece. The most beautiful effects succeed one another without confusion and ever unexpectedly; the melody is of touching solemnity; from the very first bars it imposes respect and prepares us for emotion. The rhythm becomes more bold and rollicking; the orchestration becomes richer, more sonorous, and more varied. Linked with this admirable Adagio molto is an Allegro con brio of enchanting dash. The gruppetto, a florid embellishment, found in the first measure of the theme, and given by violas and 'cellos in unison, is resumed in isolated form to establish progressions in a crescendo or in imitative passages between the winds and the strings; all these appear new and animated.

In the midst of these a melody is encountered whose first part, given out by clarinets, horns, and bassoons, concludes tutti with the rest of the orchestra; the virile energy of this melody is further enhanced by a happy choice of accompanying chords.

The Andante (marked *Larghetto* in the score) is not treated in the manner of the First Symphony. It is not composed of a subject worked out in canonic imitations, but is a pure and frank song at first sung simply by the strings, and then embroidered with rare elegance by means of light and fluent touches whose character is never far removed from the sentiment of tenderness forming the distinctive character of the principal idea. It is a ravishing picture of innocent happiness barely clouded by a few melancholy accents occurring at rare intervals.

15

The Scherzo (marked *Allegro*) is as frankly gay in its fantastic capriciousness as the second movement was fully and serenely happy. In this symphony all is smiles; the warlike bursts of the first Allegro are entirely free from violence; there is only the youthful ardor of a noble heart wherein the beautiful illusions of life are left untainted. The composer still believes in immortal glory, in love, in detachment, in self-sacrifice. What abandon in his gaiety! What wit! What impetuosity! To hear the different instruments dispute possession of a fragment of a theme not played by any one of them completely, and hearing each fragment colored with a thousand nuances as it passes from one to the other, is like watching the fairy gamboling of Oberon's graceful spirits.

The Finale — *Allegro molto* — constructed in the same manner, is a second Scherzo in double time (2/2) whose playfulness is to some extent even more refined and more piquant.

SYMPHONY NO. 3   *Eroica*   E-flat major   opus 55

first movement: *Allegro con brio*
second movement: *Marcia funebre: Adagio assai*
third movement: *Scherzo: Allegro vivace*
fourth movement: *Finale: Allegro molto; Poco andante*

The title — *Eroica* — gives us a false idea. A grave wrong has been done by truncating the inscription the composer placed at the head of his work. And it is as follows: "Heroic symphony to celebrate the anniversary of the death of a great man."

The title indicates we will find neither battles nor triumphal marches, as many might infer from its mutilated form, but grave and profound thoughts, of melancholy memories and melodies of imposing grandeur and sadness, in a word, the funeral rites of a hero. I know of no other example in music of a style wherein grief is so able to sustain itself consistently in forms of such purity and nobility of expression.

The first movement is in triple time, and at a velocity nearly equal to a waltz. Nevertheless what can be more serious or more dramatic than this Allegro? The energetic theme forming its background does not present itself completely at first. Contrary to his custom, the master gives us but a glimpse of his melodic idea. It does not present itself in its full splendor until after an introduction of a few bars. The rhythm is particularly notable for the frequency of its syncopation; and by double-measure combinations thrown into syncopated form by accenting the weak beat in the triple bar.

When rude dissonances present themselves in combination with this disjointed rhythm, like those near the middle of the second repeat, it is impossible to repress a sensation of fear at such a picture of ungovernable fury. It is the voice of despair and of rage. At the following bar the orchestra becomes calm, as if exhausted by excesses, its strength begins to

17

fail suddenly. The phrases are gentle and indicative of sad regrets. It is not possible to describe or even to hint at the multitude of melodic and harmonic aspects wherein Beethoven reproduces his theme. We will confine ourselves to mentioning one extremely strange, forming the text of many discussions, and which the French editor corrected in the score, imagining it to be the mistake of the engraver, but reinstated later on when more ample information was available.

The first and second violins in tremolo sustain the major second B-flat, A-flat (part of the chord of the dominant seventh in E-flat); when a horn, seeming to be at fault, and coming in four bars too soon, starts timidly with the beginning of the principal theme, running exclusively on the notes E-flat, G, E-flat, B-flat. One may imagine the strange effect produced by this melody formed of the three notes of the tonic chord against the two dissonant notes of the dominant, although this harshness is greatly reduced by the parts being separated.

But at the moment our ears are inclined to protest this terrible anomaly, a vigorous tutti interrupts the horn and, concluding *piano* on the tonic chord, allows the 'cellos to return to state the entire theme in its natural harmony. Considering these things from even the most elevated and detached point of view; it is difficult to find serious justification for this musical caprice.

Without doubt the master must have so intended it, as it is related that during the first rehearsal of this symphony, his friend Ries who was present, stopped the orchestra by crying out: "Very fast, as fast as possible, the horn made a mistake."*

His only reward for his indiscreet zeal was a sharp slap from the hand of the master.

No other such eccentricity is found in the rest of the score; and the Funeral March is a drama in itself. The end is especially and profoundly moving. The march theme reappears in fragments interspersed with silence, and without any other accompaniment than three notes played *pizzicato* by the double basses. When these shreds of the lugubrious melody are bare, alone, broken, and have passed one by one to the tonic, the wind instruments cry out as if it was the last goodbye of the warriors to their companions in arms. The whole orchestra dies away on an organ point played *pianissimo*.

The third movement, Scherzo, and so entitled according to Beethoven's custom, is from the Italian, meaning play or humorous frolic. At first glance it does not seem obvious how such a style can figure in such an epic

---

*Another report of the incident insists Ries cried out: "Too soon; too soon. The horn is wrong." However, all reports agree Beethoven silenced him with a buffet. Most modern listeners, who are not overawed by the rules of musical composition, find the passage to their liking, although Berlioz felt this was a whim of Beethoven amounting to absurdity.—Ed.

18

composition. To understand this it must be heard. The rhythm and the movement of the scherzo are there. But there is also play, although of the funereal kind, where at each instance clouded by thoughts of mourning, there is a kind of play recalling the warriors of the Iliad who celebrated around the tombs of their chiefs.

Beethoven knew, even in the most capricious evolutions of his orchestra, how to preserve the grave and somber tints as well as the profound sadness which should dominate.

The Finale is nothing but the development of the same poetic idea. One very curious instrumental passage occurs at the outset, revealing to what effect the various timbres contribute in opposition. It is the B-flat taken up by the violins; repeated by the flutes and oboes as an echo. Although this repercussion takes place on the same note of the scale, at the same movement, and with equal force, such a great difference results from this dialog that the distinguishing nuance of the instruments might be compared to that nuance between blue and violet. Such refinements of tone were entirely unknown before Beethoven; we owe them to him alone.

The Finale, although so varied, consists entirely of a very simple fugato theme upon which the composer builds, in addition to many ingenious details, two other themes. One of the latter is of extreme beauty. The outline of this melody does not make it possible to see, so to speak, what has been extracted from another. On the contrary, its expression is much more touching, and it is incomparably more graceful than the first theme, its character is somewhat like a bass, and a function it fulfills very well. This melody reappears shortly before the end, more slowly, with new harmonies, and with an increased effect of its sadness.

The hero causes us many tears, but after the last regrets are paid to his memory, the poet turns from elegy to intone this hymn of glory. It may appear somewhat laconic, but this peroration rises to a high point, and crowns this musical monument.

Beethoven has written works more striking than this symphony, and several of his other compositions impress the public in a more lively way. But it must be allowed, nevertheless, the *Sinfonia eroica* possesses such strength of thought and execution, in a style so emotional and so consistently elevated, besides its form being so poetical, it is entitled to rank as equal to the highest conceptions of its composer.

A sentiment of not only grave but ancient sadness overcomes me whenever I hear this symphony, although the public seems indifferently touched by it. We must certainly deplore the misfortune of an artist who, consumed by such enthusiasm, fails to make himself well enough understood, even by a refined audience, to ensure his hearers will be raised to the level of his own inspiration. It is all the more sad when the same audience, on other occasions, becomes ardent, excited, or sorrowful along with him. It becomes seized with a real and lively passion for some of his compositions, admittedly equally admirable, but nevertheless not more beautiful than this work.

Such an audience appreciates at its just value the A-minor Allegretto of the Seventh Symphony; the Allegretto scherzando of the Eighth; the Finale of the Fifth; and the Scherzo of the Ninth. It even appears to experience emotion at the Funeral March of the symphony we are now discussing — the *Eroica;* but respecting the first movement it is impossible to indulge in any illusion. Twenty years of observation tend to assure me the public listens to it with a feeling approaching coldness; and appears to recognize in it a learned and an energetic composition, but nothing more.

No philosophy is applicable to this instance; for it is useless to say it has always been so, and the same fate has everywhere befallen all great productions of the human mind. Or the causes of poetic emotion are secret and inappreciable; the conception of certain beauties wherein particular individuals are gifted is absolutely lacking in the multitude; or it is even impossible it should be otherwise.

All that is no consolation. It does not calm the indignation filling one's heart — an indignation instinctive, involuntary, and, perhaps even absurd — at the aspect of a misunderstood marvel; of a composition so noble being regarded by the crowd without being perceived; listened to without being understood; and allowed to pass without courting any attention, just as if it were a mere instance of something mediocre or indifferent.

Oh, it is frightful to be obliged to acknowledge with pitiless conviction what I find beautiful may constitute beauty for me, but it may not do so for my best friend, as he whose tastes generally correspond with my own, may be affected in a totally different manner; and even the work affording me with transports of pleasure, exciting me to the utmost, moving me to tears, may leave him cold, and may even cause him displeasure and annoyance.

Most great poets have little feeling for music, enjoying only trivial or childish melodies. Many intellectual people, who think they love it, have little idea of the emotion it is capable of raising. These are sad truths. But they are so palpably evident that nothing but the illusion caused by certain systems can stand in the way of their recognition. I have seen a dog bark with pleasure on hearing a major third, executed *sostenuto* by double stopping on the violin; but the offspring of the same animal were not in the least affected, either by the third, fifth, sixth, or octave; or in fact by any chord whatsoever — consonant or dissonant. The public, however it may be composed, is always, with respect to great musical compositions, in a similar position. It has certain nerves vibrating in sympathy with certain forms of resonance. But this organization, incomplete as it is, is distributed unequally, and is also subject to many modifications.

It would be almost foolish to count upon such and such artistic means in preference to others for the purpose of acting upon it. The composer

20

is best advised to follow blindly in his own sentiment; resigning himself beforehand to the results chance may have in store for him.

One day I was coming out of the Conservatoire with three or four amateurs; the occasion being a performance of the Choral Symphony.

"What do you think of that work?" said one of them to me.

"Immense! Magnificent! Overpowering!"

"That is singular. For my part I found it cruelly tiresome. And you?" added the speaker addressing an Italian.

"Oh, as for me, I find it obscure, or rather unpleasant, for there is no melody."

But besides these, observe the various views several journals express: "The Choral Symphony of Beethoven represents the culminating point of modern music. Art has hitherto produced nothing to be compared with it in respect to nobleness of style, grandeur of plan, and refinement of detail."

Another journal: "The Choral Symphony of Beethoven is a monstrosity."

Another: "This work is not altogether lacking in ideas; but these are badly disposed; and the general effect is incoherent, and devoid of charm."

Another: "The Choral Symphony of Beethoven contains some admirable passages; although it is evident the composer lacked ideas, and his exhausted imagination no longer sustaining him, he made considerable effort, and often with some success, to replace inspiration with artistic resources. The few phrases met within it are handled in a superior manner, and are disposed in a perfectly clear and logical order. On the whole it is the highly interesting work of a used-up genius."

Where shall we find the truth, or where shall we find the error? Everywhere and yet in no particular place. Each one is right, as what is beautiful for one is not so for another. This naturally follows, if only from the fact one has experienced emotion whereas the other has remained unaffected. The first received lively enjoyment while the second suffered intense fatigue. What can be done in such a case? Nothing. But it is distressing, and it makes me feel inclined to prefer the foolish view of beauty being absolute.

SYMPHONY NO. 4   B-flat major   opus 60

first movement: *Adagio; Allegro vivace*
second movement: *Adagio*
third movement: *Allegro vivace*
fourth movement: *Allegro ma non troppo*

Here Beethoven abandons ode and elegy entirely to return to the less lofty and less somber but no less difficult style of the Second Symphony. The general character of this score is either lively, alert, and gay, or of celestial sweetness. Except for the meditative Adagio, serving as its introduction, the first movement is almost completely given over to joy.

The motive in detached notes, opening the Allegro vivace, is only a background where the composer is later enabled to show off other melodies of more real character. The effect of the latter imparts a secondary character to what apparently was the principal idea at the outset.

This artifice, although fertile in curious and interesting results, was used by Mozart and Haydn with considerable success. But in the second part of the same Allegro vivace we find a really new idea. The first few bars alert us, and after its mysterious developments catch the listener's attention, its unexpected conclusion strikes him with astonishment.

It is composed as follows: after a fairly vigorous *tutti* the first violins offer the original theme by carrying on a pianissimo dialogue with the second violins. This ends with holding notes in the dominant chord of B natural, each instance of such holding notes is followed by two bars of silence broken only by a light kettledrum roll.

After two such entrances the kettledrum stops to allow the strings a chance to sweetly murmur other fragments of the theme. The kettledrum now returns and continues the roll for some twenty bars. The force of tonality possessed by this B flat, at first barely apparent, becomes greater as the kettledrum roll continues. After this the other instruments add to the

23

onward march by slight and unfinished bits, preparing us for a continuous roll of the kettledrum on a general *forte* where the perfect chord of B flat is finally stated in all its majesty by the full orchestra.

This remarkable crescendo is one of the best conceived effects we know of in all music; and its counterpart can scarely be found elsewhere except in a similar feature where the celebrated scherzo of the C-minor symphony, Beethoven's fifth, is concluded. The latter, notwithstanding its immense effect, is conceived on a scale less vast, starting from *piano* to arrive at the final explosion without departing from the original key.

The episode we are now describing, on the other hand, starts mezzoforte, is later lost for a moment in a pianissimo while harmonized in a manner always vague and undecided. Then it reappears with chords of a more settled tonality, and bursts forth only at a moment when the cloud enshrouding the modulation has disappeared completely. It might be compared to a river whose peaceful waters suddenly disappear, and only emerge from their underground bed to form a furious and foaming waterfall.

The Adagio eludes all analysis. Its form is so pure, and the expression of its melancholy is so angelic, and of such irresistible tenderness, that the prodigious art wherein this perfection is attained disappears completely. From the very first we are overtaken by an emotion, becoming so overpowering in its intensity near the close, that only among the giants of poetic art can we find anything comparable to this sublime page of the giant of music.

Nothing more resembles the impression produced by this Adagio than what is experienced when reading the touching episode of Francesca di Rimini in the *Divine Comedy*. Virgil could not hear its recital without sobbing bitterly; and its last line causes Dante to collapse like a corpse.

The Scherzo (*Allegro vivace*) consists almost entirely of double-rhythm phrases forcibly forming triple-time combinations. This device, often used by Beethoven, gives verve to the style; melodic outlines become sharper and more surprising. These rhythms, running counter to the ordinary beat, present a charm all of their own. This is very real although difficult to explain. Pleasure results from this disturbance of the normal accent, regaining its position at the close of each phrase. The sense of the musical discourse, suspended for a while, arrives at a complete and satisfactory conclusion.

The melody of the trio, confined to the woodwinds, is of delicious freshness. Its movement is slower than the rest of the Scherzo; and its elegant simplicity is enhanced by meeting the opposition of short phrases coming from the violins, seeming to cast upon the surface of the harmony similar charming traits of innocent mischief.

The Finale (*Allegro ma non troppo*), gay and sprightly, returns to ordinary rhythmic forms. It is an animated swarm of sparkling notes caus-

24

ing a continuous babble. It is interrupted, however, by occasional rough and uncouth chords, where the angry outbursts, already mentioned as peculiar to this composer, are again evident.

SYMPHONY NO. 5　　　　C minor　　　　opus 67
first movement: *Allegro con brio*
second movement: *Andante con moto*
third movement: *Allegro*
fourth movement: *Allegro*

The most celebrated symphony of all, is also in our opinion, without question the one where Beethoven gives free scope to his vast imagination, without choosing to be guided or supported by any exterior thought.

In the first, second, and fourth symphonies he uses more or less extended forms already known; investing them with the poetry of the brilliant and passionate inspiration stemming from his vigorous youth. In the third (*Eroica*) the form tends to broaden, it is true; the thought also attains a greater height.

However, notwithstanding all this, we cannot fail to recognize therein the influence of one or another of those divine poets to whom the great artist had long erected a temple within his heart.

Beethoven, faithful to the precept of Horace:

> *Vos exemplaria Graeca*
> *Nocturna versate manu,*
> *versate diurna.*
>
> Make Greece your model when you write,
> and turn her volumes over day and night.

used to read Homer habitually and, in his magnificent musical epic — rightly or wrongly said to be inspired by a modern hero — remembrances of the ancient Iliad play an admirable but no less evident part.

The Symphony in C minor (the Fifth), on the other hand, appears to come directly from Beethoven's genius. His own intimate thoughts are developed there; as well as his secret sorrows, his pent-up rages, his dreams filled with melancholy oppression, his nocturnal visions, and his bursts of

27

enthusiasm furnish its entire subject; whereas the melodic, harmonic, rhythmic, and orchestral forms are delineated with an essential novelty and individuality also giving them considerable power and nobility.

The first movement is devoted to the expression of the disordered sentiments filling a great soul when it is preyed upon by despair. It is not the calm and concentrated despair bearing the outward look of resignation; or the grief so similar and silent shown by Romeo when hearing of Juliet's death. Rather it is the terrible fury of Othello when hearing from Iago's mouth the poisoned calumnies persuading him of Desdemona's crime.

Sometimes it is an excessive depression, expressing itself only in accents of regret, and appearing to hold itself in pity. Listen to those orchestral gasps; to those chords in the dialogue between woodwinds and strings, coming and going while gradually growing weaker like the painful breathing of a dying man.

These finally give place to a phrase full of violence where the orchestra seems to rise again as if animated by a spark of fury. Look at that quivering mass, hesitating for an instant, and then precipitating itself bodily divided into two ardent unisons resembling two streams of lava. And, having done this, say whether this passionate style is not beyond and above anything yet produced in instrumental music.

The movement presents a striking example of the effect produced by the excessive doubling of parts under certain circumstances, and of the wild aspect of the chord of the fourth on the second note of the scale, sometimes described as the second inversion of the chord of the dominant. It is often encountered without preparation or resolution, and even occurs once without the leading note and on an organ point; the D forming the bass of the strings while the G forms the discordant summit of a few parts assigned to the woodwinds.

The Adagio (*Andante con moto*) presents a characteristic relationship to the A-minor Allegretto in the Seventh Symphony, and to that in E flat in the Fourth Symphony. It offers equally the melancholy gravity of the former and the touching grace of the latter. The theme, first stated by the 'cellos and the violas, along with a simple pizzicato double-bass accompaniment, is followed by a certain phrase for the woodwinds, recurring continually in the same form and key from one end to the other of this movement, whatever the successive modification of the original theme.

This persistence of one and the same phrase in always adhering to its original simplicity is so profoundly sad it gradually produces upon the soul of the listener an impression impossible to describe although certainly the most powerful of its kind we have ever experienced.

At the last entry of the original theme there is also a canon in unison at a bar's distance between violins and flutes, clarinets, and bassoons. This would give the melody so treated a new interest, if it were possible to hear the imitation of the woodwinds, but unfortunately the orchestra is then playing so loud it is made inaudible.

28

The Scherzo (the third movement, marked *Allegro*) is a strange composition; its first bars, although presenting nothing terrible, cause the strange emotion we experience under the magnetic glance of certain individuals. Everything in it is mysterious and somber. The orchestral devices appear somewhat sinister, appearing to belong to the same order of ideas creating the famous Bloksberg scene in Goethe's *Faust*.

Piano and *mezzoforte* tints prevail. The middle part, or trio, is remarkable for a brass passage executed with all the force of the bow. Its uncouth weight shakes the feet of the player's music stands, and somewhat resembles the frolicking of a jolly elephant. But the monster departs, and the noise of his mad careening dies away gradually. The scherzo motive reappears pizzicato; peace is regained gradually until nothing more is heard than a few notes plucked daintily by the violins, plus the strange clucking of the bassoons giving their high A flat closely opposed by G as octave in the chord of the dominant minor ninth.

Then the strings, *col arco,* interrupting the cadence, softly take the A-flat chord as their resting place for a bit. The rhythm depends entirely on the kettledrum, and is sustained by light strokes struck by sponge-covered sticks, forming a dull design against the stagnation of the rest of the orchestra.

The kettledrum note is C, whereas the key of the movement is C minor; but the A-flat chord, long sustained by other instruments, seems on one hand to introduce a different tonality, while on the other the isolated martellato of the kettledrum on C tends to preserve the spirit of the original key.

The ear hesitates, uncertain as to how this harmonic mystery is about to resolve itself, when the dull pulsations of the kettledrum, becoming more and more intense, meet the violins who have rejoined the rhythmic movement and changed the harmony. The chord is now the dominant seventh (G, B, D, F) where the kettledrum stubbornly continues its roll upon the C tonic.

And then the entire orchestra, reinforced by the trombones which have not appeared before, bursts forth in the major mode on a triumphal march theme, and the finale begins.

Everyone knows the effect of this thunderstroke; it is useless, therefore, to detain the reader with any further comment.

Nevertheless the critics have tried to detract from the composer's merit by declaring that in the foregoing he resorted to a mere vulgar device; the brightness of the major mode pompously succeeding the obscurity of the minor pianissimo. They also complain the triumphal theme lacks originality; and the interest grows less as the end approaches instead of following the contrary order.

We may reply to this by asking: was less genius needed to create such a work because of the passage from *piano* to *forte,* and the one from minor to major, were means already known?

29

How many other composers resorted to the same means, and how far can the results they obtained be compared to this gigantic song of victory where the soul of the poet-musician, henceforth free from all hindrance and earthly suffering, appears to rise glowing toward the very heavens?

The first four bars of the theme are, it is true, not of great originality; but the forms of the fanfare are naturally restricted; and we do not believe it would be possible to discover new ones without emerging entirely from the simple, grand, and majestic character belonging to this theme.

Beethoven, therefore, needed only a fanfare entrance for his finale; and throughout the rest of the movement, and even in the principal phrase, he retains the elevation and novelty of style which never abandons him.

Concerning the reproach of his not having proceeded with an increasing interest to the conclusion, the following may be said:

Music cannot, in the state we know it, produce a more violent effect than the transition from the scherzo to the triumphal march. It was, therefore, quite impossible to proceed with its augmentation.

To sustain such a heightened effect is in fact already a prodigious effort. Notwithstanding the developments indulged in by Beethoven, he has succeeded in accomplishing this. But this very equality between the commencement and the conclusion is enough to cause a suspicion of decrease because of the terrible shock the listener's nerves experience at the opening. Nervous emotion, thereby raised to its most violent paroxysm, becomes that much more difficult to effect immediately afterward.

In a long row of columns of equal height an optical illusion causes those farthest away to appear smaller than the rest. Perhaps our feeble organization would be better suited to a laconic peroration such as *Notre général vous rappelle** by Gluck. The audience would not have to grow cold, and the symphony would finish before fatigue had intervened to stop the possibility of accompanying the composer in his advance.

This observation, however, belongs only to the stage setting of the work; and by no means prevents the finale from being of a magnificence and a richness in comparison with which there are few pieces which could appear without being crushed completely.

*Our general calls us to muster.

SYMPHONY NO. 6   *Pastoral*   F major   opus 68
first movement: *Allegro ma non troppo* (Awakening of Serene
    Impressions on Arriving in the Country)
second movement: *Andante molto moto* (Scene by the Brook-
    side)
third movement: *Allegro* (Jolly Gathering of Countryfolk);
    Allegro (Thunderstorm; Tempest)
fourth movement: *Allegretto* (Shepherd's Song; Glad and
    Thankful Feelings After the Storm)

This astonishing landscape appears as if the joint work of Poussin and Michaelangelo. A desire to depict the calm of the countryside and the shepherd's gentle ways now actuates the composer of *Fidelio* and the *Eroica*. But let us understand each other; here are no gaily dressed shepherds of de Florian, still less those of Lebrun, author of *Rossignol,* or those of Jean-Jacques Rousseau, author of *Devin de Village.* The theme is nature in all its simple truth.

The composer titles his first movement: "Awakening of Serene Impressions on Arriving in the Country."

Herdsmen begin to appear in the fields. They have their usual careless manner; and the sound of their pipes comes from far and near. Delightful phrases greet you like the perfumed morning breeze; swarms of chattering birds in flight pass rustling overhead. From time to time the air seems charged with mist; great clouds appear and hide the sun; then, all at once, they disappear; and a torrent of sunlight falls upon the trees and the woods. That is the effect, it seems to me, upon hearing this movement; and I believe the vagueness of instrumental expression notwithstanding, many listeners have been impressed the same way.

Farther on there is a "Scene by the Brookside." It is devoted to con-

31

templation. No doubt the author created this admirable Adagio while reclining on the grass, gazing upwards, listening to the wind, fascinated by the surrounding soft reflections of light and sound; at the same time looking at and listening to the tiny white waves as they sparkled along and, with a slight murmur, broke upon the pebbles of the brink. It is indeed beautiful.

Some berate Beethoven for having tried to reproduce the songs of three birds at the end of the Adagio (second movement — *Andante molto moto* — "Scene by the Brookside"). In my opinion the absurdity or otherwise of such attempts is decided by their success or their failure. I may tell the adverse critics in this instance that their stricture appears justifiable as far as the nightingale is concerned, as this bird's song is scarcely better imitated here than in the famous flute solo of M. Lebrun; for the simple reason the nightingale only emits sounds inappreciable and variable, so these cannot be rendered with instruments having fixed tones playing in a certain key.

It seems to me this does not apply to either the cuckoo or the quail; their respective cries are two notes in one instance, and one in the other — notes true and determined, and therefore admitting to exact and complete imitation.

If the musician is now to be accused of childishness because he exactly renders the songs of birds in a scene where the calm voices of heaven, earth, and waterfall naturally find their places, I may reply the same objection could also be addressed to him when in a storm he applies similar treatment to the wind, to claps of thunder, or to the bellowing of cattle. Providence alone can tell if it ever entered the head of one of these critics to blame the storm of the Pastoral Symphony.

But let us continue. The poet now leads us into the midst of a "Jolly Gathering of Countryfolk." They laugh and dance in moderation at first, while from the oboe comes a gay refrain accompanied by a bassoon seeming able to intone only two notes. Beethoven probably intended this to represent some good old German peasant mounted on a barrel and armed with a dilapidated instrument from which he succeeds in drawing the two principal notes of the key of F — its tonic and its dominant.

Each time the oboe gives out its musettelike melody, appearing as simple and gay as a young girl dressed in her Sunday clothes, the old bassoon brings out his two notes. Should the melodic phrase modulate in the least, the bassoon is silent, quietly counting his rests until the return of the principal key allows him to come in again with an imperturbable F, C. F. This effect, so excellently grotesque, seems to almost completely escape the attention of the public.

The dance becomes more animated, excited, and noisy. The rhythm changes; and a melody in double time announces the arrival of the heavily booted mountaineers. The portion in triple time now recommences more

32

animatedly than ever. The whole becomes confused and gathers force; flowing locks begin to fall upon the shoulders of the countrywomen; the mountaineers have brought with them a wine-inspired and demonstrative joy. They clap their hands, they shout, they run and tumble — there is a climax of excitement.

But all at once comes the distant thunder, spreading fear throughout the company of this rustic ball, and all the dancers take flight.

"Thunderstorm; Tempest": I despair of being able to give an idea of this prodigious movement. It must be heard to form an idea of the degree of truth and sublimity descriptive music can attain in the hands of a man like Beethoven. Listen — listen to those rain-charged squalls of wind; to those dull grumblings of the basses; also to the keen whistling of the piccolo telling us the horrible tempest is about to break loose. The hurricane approaches and grows in force. An immense chromatic feature, starting from the heights of the instrumentation runs its course until it gropes its way to the lowest orchestral depths. There it secures the basses, dragging them with it upwards, the whole shuddering like a whirlwind sweeping all before it. Then the trombones burst forth. The thunder of the kettledrums becomes redoubled in violence.

It is no longer merely rain and wind but an awful cataclysm, the universal deluge, the end of the world.

This literally produces giddiness; and many people when they hear this storm can hardly tell if their emotion is one of pleasure or of pain.

The symphony concludes with "Shepherd's Song; Glad and Thankful Feelings After the Storm" when all resumes its cheerfulness. The shepherds reappear upon the mountains, calling together their scattered flocks. The sky is serene; the rain is almost gone; and calm returns. With its reappearance we again hear those rustic songs whose gentle melody offers us such repose to the spirit after the consternation and shock produced by the magnificent horror of the previous picture.

After that can anyone really consider it necessary to allude to any strangeness of style met with in this gigantic work? Shall we take exception to the five-note groups of 'cellos opposed to those of four notes in the double basses who jostle each other without ever subsiding together? Must we exclaim about the horn call arpeggioing the chord of C while the strings hold that of F?

Really I can't do it. For such a task one must reason coldly; and how can we be guaranteed against excitement when the mind is preoccupied with such a subject. Far from that one would like to go to sleep for entire months so as to live in imagination in that unknown sphere where genius has given us a momentary glimpse. If unfortunately we were obliged after such a concert to attend either a comic opera, or a soirée of fashionable songs or flute concertos, the effect would make one feel quite stupid regarding the question:

33

"How did you like the Italian duet?"
You might answer gravely: "Very fine."
"And those clarinet variations?"
"Superb."
"And the finale of the new opera?"
"Admirable."

Any distinguished artist who might happen to hear these answers, without knowing the cause of your preoccupation, would be certain to think: "Who is that madman?"

Ancient poems, however beautiful and admired they may be, pale into insignificance when compared with this marvel of modern music. But this poem of Beethoven — these long phrases so richly colored — these living pictures — these perfumes — that light — that eloquent silence — that vast horizon — these enchanted nooks secreted in the woods — those golden harvests — those rose-tinted clouds like wandering flocks on the surface of the sky — that immense plain seeming to slumber under the rays of the midday sun.

Man is absent, and nature alone reveals itself to admiration, and this profound repose of every living thing. This happy life of all at rest. The little brook running rippling towards the river. The river itself, parent of waters, flowing down to the great sea in majestic silence.

Then man intervenes; he of the fields, robust and god fearing. His joyous diversion is interrupted by the storm, and we have his terror and his hymn of gratitude.

Veil your faces, you poor, great, ancient poets — poor immortals. Your conventional diction with all its harmonious purity can never do battle with the art of sounds. You are glorious but vanquished.

You never knew what we call melody; harmony; the association of different tone qualities; instrumental coloring; modulation; the learned conflict of discordant sounds, first engaging in combat only to then embrace; our musical surprises; and those strange accents setting in vibration the most unexplored depths of the human soul.

The stammerings of the childlike art you called music could give you no idea of this. You alone were the great melodists and harmonists — the masters of rhythm and expression for the celebrated spirits of your time.

But these words have in all your tongues a meaning quite different from what is now their due. The art of sounds, correctly so called and independent of all else, was born yesterday. It is hardly of age with its adolescence. It is all powerful; it is the Pythian Apollo of the moderns. We are indebted to it for a whole world of feelings and sensations from which you were shut out entirely.

Yes, great and adored poets, you are conquered: *Inclyte sed victi.**

*You are glorious but vanquished.

34

SYMPHONY NO. 7   A major   opus 92
first movement: *Poco sostenuto; Vivace*
second movement: *Allegretto*
third movement: *Presto*
fourth movement: *Allegro con brio*

The Seventh Symphony is celebrated for its Allegretto (called Adagio or Andante). This does not come about because the other three movements are less worthy of admiration — far from it. But the public does not generally judge by any other yardstick than the effect produced; and it only measures this effect by the amount of applause. It follows that whatever is most applauded always passes for being the most beautiful; although these are beauties of infinite worth but not of a nature to excite any demonstrations of approval. Then, to further promote the object of this predilection, all the rest is sacrificed. In France, at least, this is the universal custom. That is why in speaking of Beethoven one says the Storm of the Pastoral (or Sixth Symphony), the Finale of the C minor (the Fifth), the Andante of the Symphony in A major (the Seventh), and so forth.

It does not seem to be certain the latter was composed after the *Pastoral* or *Eroica* symphonies. Several authorities hold to the contrary that it preceded these symphonies. The mere number designating it as seventh would, therefore, should this opinion be well founded, refer merely to the order of publication.

The first movement opens with a broad and pompous introduction where melody, modulations, and orchestral designs compete successively for the listener's interest; besides commencing with one of those instrumental effects which Beethoven was incontestibly the creator. The entire orchestral mass, striking a chord both loud and short, discovers an oboe during the succeeding silence. This oboe's entrance, hidden by the orchestral attack, had not been apparent before, and now gives the opening melody in sostenuto. No more original opening could be imagined.

35

At the end of the introduction the note E (dominant of A), recalled after several excursions into nearby keys, becomes the object of a play of tone color between violins and flutes, somewhat like that encountered in the first few bars of the finale of the *Eroica.* The E comes and goes without accompaniment during six bars; changing its aspect each time it passes from the strings to the woodwinds. Finally, held by the flute and the oboe, it joins the introduction to the Allegro, becoming the first note of the main theme, gradually outlining the rhythmical form.

I have heard this subject ridiculed because of its rustic simplicity. Probably the reproach of it lacking nobility would never have been made if the composer, as in the *Pastoral,* placed this inscription in plain letters at the head of his Allegro: "Peasants' Rondo."

We see, therefore, if these are the listeners who prefer not to be warned of the subject treated by the musician, there are others, on the contrary, who are not disposed to welcome any idea presented to them in this unaccustomed garb, unless they are told beforehand of the reason for this anomaly. In default of being able to decide between two such dissimilar opinions, it appears the artist, in such an instance, can do no better than follow his own feelings without foolishly straining to attain the chimera of popular approval.

The phrase in question is of a rhythm strongly marked. After passing to the harmony it is reproduced in a multitude of aspects without arresting its cadenced march until the end. The use of a rhythmic form in ostinato has never been attempted with so much success; and in this Allegro (first movement marked Vivace), whose extensive development runs constantly upon the same idea, it is treated with such inconceivable sagacity, the tonality changes are so frequent and so ingenious, the chords are formed into groups and chains of such novelty, that the movement concludes before the attention and ardent emotion it excites in the listener have time to lose any of their extreme vivacity.

Let us not forget before going to the next movement, to mention the curious crescendo Beethoven uses to reintroduce his favorite rhythm, one he had abandoned for an instant. It is produced by a two-bar phrase repeated eleven times in succession by the basses and the violas in a low pitch, while the woodwinds hold E above, below, and in the middle, in quadruple octave; and while the violins keep delivering, as a kind of chime, the notes E, A, E, C sharp, whose percussions continually increase in tempo and are combined to present the dominant when the basses are at D or B sharp; and after either the tonic or its third, whenever they play C sharp. This is absolutely new; and no imitator has, I think, yet attempted to apply this lovely discovery very happily.

The rhythm, as simple as that of the first movement, although of different form, is equally the chief cause of the incredible effect produced by the Allegretto. It consists exclusively of a dactyl followed by a spondee,

36

occurring without stopping, sometimes in three parts, sometimes in a single part, and sometimes in all the parts in unison. Sometimes they serve as an accompaniment, often attracting a concentrated attention to themselves, or furnishing the first theme of a small episodic double fugue for the strings. It first appears for the lower strings of the violas, 'cellos, and double basses, marked *piano;* with the intention of being repeated shortly thereafter in a pianissimo full of melancholy and mystery.

From there it passes to the second violins, while the 'cellos chant a kind of lamentation in the minor mode; the rhythmical phrases rising continually from octave to octave, and thereby arriving at the pitch of the first violins. These, by means of a crescendo, transmit it to the woodwinds in the upper region of the orchestra where it then explodes in all its force. Thereupon the melodious plaint, being stated with greater energy, takes on the character of a convulsive lamentation; irreconcilable rhythms agitate painfully one against another — these are the tears, the sobs, the supplications, in short, the expression of unlimited grief and of a devouring form of suffering.

But a gleam of hope has just appeared; these agonizing accents are followed by an airy melody: pure, simple, soft, and resigned — patience smiling at grief. Only the basses continue their inexorable rhythm under this rainbow of melody; and it seems, if I may borrow a quotation from English poetry, like:

One fatal remembrance, one sorrow, that throws
Its black shade alike o'er our joys and our woes.

The orchestra, after a few alternations reminiscent of anguish and resignation, as if fatigued by such a painful struggle, presents only fragments of the original theme, and dies away exhausted. The flutes and oboes take up the theme with a murmuring voice, but they lack the strength to finish it; and the ending falls to the violins in a few barely perceptible pizzicato notes. After this with a flicker of fresh animation, reminding one of the flame of a lamp about to die out, the woodwinds exhale a profound sigh upon an indecisive harmony, and all is silence. This plaintive explanation, commencing and concluding the Andante (Allegretto), is produced by a six-four chord, continually tending to resolve on some other; and its incomplete harmonic sense is the only one allowing its use for the purpose of finishing in a manner leaving the hearer with a vague impression and augmenting the feeling of dreamy sadness where all of the preceding must have plunged him.

The Scherzo's (*Presto*) subject is modeled in quite a new style. It is in F major; and instead of concluding its first section in C, or B flat, or D minor, or A minor, or A flat, or D flat, like most pieces of this kind, the modulation finally falls on the key of its third — A major. The scherzo of the Pastoral Symphony, also in F, modulates into D major — a third lower. There is some resemblance in the color presented in this contrast

37

of keys; but this is not the only affinity existing between the two works. The trio of the present movement (*Presto meno assai*), where the violins hold the dominant almost continually, while the oboes and clarinets perform a genial rustic melody, is completely within the idea of the landscape and the idyll. We also meet in it a new form of crescendo, given in a lower part by the second horn, murmuring two notes: A and G sharp in double time, although the bar is of three beats and accentuates the G sharp although A is the integral note. The public always seems struck with astonishment when hearing this passage.

The Finale (*Allegro con brio*) is as rich as the foregoing movement in new combinations, piquant modulations, and capricious charm. The theme presents a certain relationship with that of the overture of *Armide,* but only in the arrangement of the first four notes, and this is more evident to the eye than to the ear; for when executed nothing can be more different than these two ideas.

We should better appreciate the freshness and coquetry of Beethoven's phrases, so different from the cavalier spirit of Gluck's theme, if the chords taken in upper parts by the woodwinds were less dominating over the first violins singing in the middle register, while the second violins and violas accompany the melody below with a double-stopped tremolo.

Beethoven, throughout the course of the Finale, has drawn effects as graceful as they are unforeseen from the key of C-sharp minor to that of D major. One of the happiest bold harmonic strokes is, without question, the great pedal on the dominant E set off by a D sharp of a value equal to that of the principal note. The chord of the seventh is also introduced in a way the D natural of the upper part falls precisely upon the D sharp of the basses. One might expect this to result in a horrible discord; or in a deficiency in the clarity of the harmony. Nothing of the kind happens, however; the tonal force of the dominant is such that the D sharp affects it not at all; and the bourdon of E continues to be heard exclusively. Beethoven did not write his music merely to have it looked at.

The coda, introduced by this threatening pedal, is of extraordinary brightness, and well worthy of terminating such a masterpiece of technical ability, taste, fantasy, knowledge, and inspiration.

SYMPHONY NO. 8   F major   opus 93

first movement: *Allegro vivace e con brio*
second movement: *Allegretto scherzando*
third movement: *Tempo di menuetto*
fourth movement: *Allegro vivace*

This symphony is in F, like the *Pastoral* (the Sixth), but it is conceived within less vast proportions than its predecessors. But if it scarcely surpasses in amplitude of form the First Symphony in C, it is far superior to it in instrumentation, rhythm, and melodic style.

The first movement contains two subjects; both are gentle and calm. The second subject, in our opinion the more remarkable, seems to constantly avoid the perfect cadences by modulating in a wholly unexpected way (the phrase starts in D and ends in C) and then disappears without any conclusion on the chord of the diminished seventh.

When hearing this melodic caprice it almost seems as if the author, although desiring a gentle emotion, had suddenly been prevented from continuing his happy song by the intervention of some sad thought.

The Andante scherzando (*Allegretto scherzando*) is one of those productions where it is equally vain to seek either a model or a counterpart; seeming to have fallen from heaven and to have immediately entered the composer's mind; he therefore writes, as it were, at a stroke; and we can only listen to it with amazement. Here the woodwinds play a part not usually falling their lot. In other words they accompany, with added chords, repeated eight times pianissimo in each bar, the light *punta d'arco* dialogue of the violins and the basses. It is soft and ingenious, also being of an especially graceful laziness like the song of two children gathering flowers in a meadow on a beautiful spring morning.

Two three-bar sections form the principal phrase whose symmetry is disturbed by the silence succeeding the bass reply. The first section ends on a weak beat, and the second on a strong one. The chord repetitions of the oboes, clarinets, horns, and bassoons are so interesting the listener seems prevented from observing the symmetrical defect produced in the cantabile of the strings by the quantity of added silence.

The addition referred to apparently exists only to allow the delightful chord to take flight so it can be heard alone and longer. By this example we again see the law of strict outline may sometimes be infringed upon with success; but it can be believed this ravishing idyll ends by the very one of all common features Beethoven had the greatest aversion — the Italian cadence.

At the moment the instrumental conversation of the two little orchestras, woodwind and string, is most attractive, the composer, as if suddenly compelled to finish, makes the violins play four notes in tremolo: G — sixth, F — dominant, A — leading note, B flat — tonic; repeats them several times, just like the Italians when they sing Fe – li – ci – tà, and then stops short. I have never been able to explain this comical ending to myself.

A minuet, with all the style and exact movement of Haydn's minuets, replaces the quick triple-time scherzo Beethoven invented and made such ingenious and attractive use of in all his other symphonic compositions. To speak truthfully, this movement is ordinary; and the antiquity of its form seems to have stifled the composer's thought.

The finale, on the contrary, sparkles with animation; its ideas are brilliant, new, and are developed luxuriously. Diatonic progressions are found in two parts and in contrary motion; serving the composer in creating a crescendo of tremendous extent and grand effect for his peroration. The harmony includes a few instances of harshness produced by the resolution of passing notes not being sufficiently prompt; and by passing notes sometimes stopping short before a rest.

These passing discords can be explained easily by slightly straining the mere letter of theoretical law; but in performance they always produce an effect more or less unpleasant.

A contrary example is given by the high pedal of the flutes and oboes on F, while the kettledrums, tuned in the octave, hammer out the same note below the reentry of the theme; the violins playing: C, G, B flat of the chord of the dominant seventh, preceded by the third F, A, fragment of the tonic chord.

I insist this sustained upper note, forbidden theoretically as it forms no part of the harmony, gives no offense. Far from it, thanks to an adroit disposition of the instruments, and to the peculiar character of the phrase, the result of this aggregation of sound is excellent and of remarkable sweetness.

Before concluding we must not omit to mention a certain orchestral effect, the one that most surprises the listener during the performance of this finale. We refer to the C-sharp note struck loudly by the entire mass of instruments in unison an octave after a diminuendo just dying away on C natural.

The roar of sound is followed immediately, the first two times, by a return of the theme in F. This shows the C sharp was really enharmonically a D flat, chromatically altered from the sixth note of the scale. However, the third appearance of this strange return bears a different aspect. The orchestra, modulating to C as before, now strikes a real D flat followed by a fragment of the theme in that key. Then an equally genuine C sharp comes, succeeded by another part of the theme in C-sharp minor. Resuming the same C sharp, and repeating it three times with increased force, the entire theme now enters in F-sharp minor.

The same sound, figuring at the outset as a minor sixth, becomes successively at its last appearance:
1. tonic, major, flattened
2. tonic, minor, flattened
3. dominant

This is most curious.

SYMPHONY NO. 9   *Choral—Ode to Joy*   D minor   opus 125
first movement: *Allegro ma non troppo, un poco maestoso*
second movement: *Molto vivace; Presto*
third movement: *Adagio molto e cantabile*
fourth movement: *Presto; Allegro assai; Rezitativo; Allegro assai*
                  (Ode to Joy — choral finale)

To analyze such a composition is a difficult and a dangerous task, and one we have long hesitated to undertake. It is a hazardous attempt; the excuse for it can lie only in preserving efforts to place ourselves in the composer's point of view, and thereby perceive the inner meaning of his work, feel its effect, and study the impression it has produced upon privileged organizations and on the public at large. Among the many judgments on this work, perhaps not even two are identical.

Some critics regard it as a monstrous folly. Others only see in it the last gleams of an expiring genius. A few more prudent ones confess they do not yet understand it but hope to be able to appreciate it, at least somewhat, later on. The great mass of artists deem it an extraordinary conception although some of its parts are not yet explained and seem to have no direct object.

But there are a few musicians who are driven by their nature to be very careful in examining whatever may tend to increase the field of art. They have reflected maturely upon the general plan of the Choral Symphony and, after having read it and listened to it attentively on many occasions, they are firm in the conviction this work is the most magnificent expression of Beethoven's genius. That opinion, as already hinted here, is the one to which we adhere.

Without prying into what the composer wished to express in this vast musical poem in terms of ideas personal to himself, this being a search where the area of conjecture is open to all, let us see if the novelty of form is not justified here by an intention altogether independent of philosophic or religious thought, an intention as reasonable and as beautiful for the fervent Christian as for the pantheist or the atheist — in fact an intention purely musical and poetical.

Beethoven had written eight symphonies before this. What means were available to him in the event of his proposing to go beyond the point where he had already arrived by the unaided resources of instrumentation? The coupling of vocal and instrumental forces. But to observe the law of crescendo, and to place the power of the auxiliary he wished to give the orchestra in effective relief in the work itself, was it not necessary to still allow the instruments to occupy the foreground of the picture he proposed to unfold? This proposition being admitted, we can readily imagine him induced to adopt a style of mixed music capable of serving as a connecting link between the two great divisions of the symphony. The instrumental recitative became the bridge he projected between chorus and orchestra, and over this the instruments passed to become united with the voices.

The passage being decided on, the composer was obligated to make his intention clear by announcing the fusion he was about to effect. Then, speaking through the mouth of a baritone coryphée, he himself cried out, using the very notes of the instrumental recitative he had just used:
O friends, not these tones! Let us sing something more pleasant, more full of gladness.

In the foregoing lies the treaty of alliance entered into between chorus and orchestra. The same recitative phrase pronounced by one and the other appearing to be the form of an oath taken mutually. From that point the musician was free to choose the text of his choral composition. It is to Schiller that Beethoven applies. He takes the poet's *Ode to Joy,* colors it with a thousand tints the unaided poetry could never have conveyed and, right to the end, pursues one continuing road of increasing pomp, grandeur, and acclaim.

Such is probably the more or less plausible reason for the general arrangement of this immense composition whose several parts we are now about to study.

The first movement, with its imprint of somber majesty, does not resemble any Beethoven had written before. The harmony is sometimes excessively bold; and designs of the most original kind, as well as features of the most expressive order, meet, cross, and intertwine without causing obscurity or encumbrance. The general result, on the contrary, is one perfectly clear effect. The multitude of orchestral voices may complain or threaten, each in its own peculiar way or special style; but they all appear to combine in forming one single voice, so great is the strength of the sentiment animating them.

The Allegro maestoso, written in D minor, begins on the chord of A without its third, or, in other words, with a combination of A, E, placed as a fifth and arpeggioed above and below the violins, violas, and double basses so the hearer does not know if what he hears is the chord of A minor, A major, or the dominant of D. This drawn-out indecision regarding tonality gives much force and dignity of character to the tutti entry on the D-minor chord. The peroration includes accents completely stirring the soul; and it would be hard to find anything more profoundly tragic than this song of the woodwinds beneath which a tremolo chromatic phrase for the strings gradually swells and rises, grumbling like the sea as a storm approaches. This is a magnificent inspiration.

The Scherzo vivace (*Molto vivace*) following contains nothing similar. It is true we find solid pedals in it, high and medium on the tonic, and passing through the chord of the dominant. However, I have already made my profession of faith regarding these holding notes foreign to the harmony; and there is no need for this new example to prove the excellent help they can render when naturally induced by the musical sense. Beethoven, especially by means of the rhythm, was able to imbue this charming badinage with considerable interest. The theme, so full of vivacity when it presents itself with its fugal reply four bars later, literally sparkles with life when the reply, coming in a bar sooner than expected, forms a three-bar rhythmic design in lieu of the double-time beginning.

The middle of the Scherzo is taken up by a double-time presto (alla breve) of quite rural joviality; and its theme unfolds upon the tonic or dominant intermediate pedals, accompanied by a countermelody harmonizing equally well with one or the other of these two holding notes.

The song is introduced for the last time by an oboe phrase of delightful freshness; and after its having played for some time with the chord of the major ninth (dominant of D) disports itself in the key of F in a way as graceful as it is unexpected. A reflection of these gentle expressions so dear to Beethoven may be seen in this; impressions produced by nature in aspects smiling and calm, in atmospheric purity, in the first rays of dawn on a spring morn.

In the Adagio cantabile the principle of unity is so little observed it might be looked upon as two distinct pieces rather than one. The first melody in B flat and in common time is followed by another, absolutely different from it, in D and in triple time; the first theme, altered slightly and varied by the first violins, makes a second appearance in the original key, to reintroduce the melody in triple time. This appears in the key of G, without alteration or variation, the first theme then installs itself; and does not allow its rival to share the listener's attention.

Several hearings are required before one can become altogether accustomed to so singular a disposition of this marvelous adagio. Regarding the beauty of all these melodies, the infinite grace of the ornaments applied to them, the sentiments of melancholy tenderness, passionate sadness, and religious meditation they express, if my prose could render even

45

an approximate idea of all this, music would have found such a competitor in the written word that even the greatest of all poets would never be able to oppose it.

It is an immense work and, once its powerful charm is experienced, the only answer to the critic who reproaches the composer for having violated the law of unity is:

So much the worse for the law!

We are now approaching the instant when the vocal and instrumental elements are to be coupled. The 'cellos and double basses intone the recitative, already described, after a ritornello of the woodwinds as violent and rough as an angry outburst. The chord of the major sixth (F, A, D), commencing this Presto, is interrupted by an appogiatura on the B flat, struck simultaneously by flute, oboes, and clarinets. This sixth note of the key of D minor grates horribly against the dominant, and produces an exceedingly harsh effect. This is very expressive of fury and rage; but I still don't quite see what it was that so excited the composer, unless before saying to his coryphée:

Oh friends, not these tones! Let us sing something more pleasant, more full of gladness.

he wanted by some odd whim to calumnify instrumental harmony.

But he seems to regret it, for between each phrase of the bass recitative he quotes fragments of the three preceding movements as souvenirs saved in affection; and after this same recitative he places in the orchestra, amidst an exquisite choice of chords, the beautiful theme all the voices are soon to sing to Schiller's ode. This calm and gentle chant gradually becomes more animated and brilliant in passing from the basses, who first announce it, to the strings and woodwinds. After a sudden interruption the entire orchestra resumes the furious ritornello announcing the vocal recitative.

The first chord is again on F, supposed to carry the third and the sixth. It really carries them; but this time the composer is not contented with the B-flat appogiatura as he adds E, G, and C sharp so all the notes of the major diatonic scale are played together and produce F, A, C sharp, E, G, B flat, D — a frightful assemblage.

Martin, the French composer called Martini, wanted in his opera *Sappho,* written about forty years ago, to produce a similar effect by simultaneously using every diatonic, chromatic, and enharmonic interval. This occurs at the moment when Phaon's lover is about to throw herself into the waves; and without worrying about the suitability of such an attempt, and without inquiring whether or not this was an infringement on the dignity of art, we may be sure his object was not misunderstood. My efforts to discover that of Beethoven would be completely useless. I see a formal intention, a calculated and thought-out project, producing two chords at the two instants preceding the successive appearances of vocal and instrumental recitative. Although I have searched high and low for the reason behind this idea, I am forced to admit it is unknown to me.

The coryphée having sung his recitative, whose words are by Beethoven himself, as we have remarked, alone delivers the *Ode to Joy* theme, accompanied lightly by two wind instruments and strings pizzicato. This theme appears up to the end of the symphony, and is always recognizable even though its form changes continually. The study of these various transformations is extremely interesting as each one imparts a new and definite tint to the expression of the same sentiment — joy.

At first this joy is full of gentleness and peace but the moment the female voices make themselves heard it becomes more lively. The time changes; the phrase first sung in 4/4 becomes 6/8 and, with continual syncopation, when it takes on a stronger character, it becomes more agile and in general approaches a warlike style.

This is the song of the hero certain of victory. We can almost see his armor sparkle, and hear the sound of his measured tread. A fugato theme, where the original design may still be traced, temporarily furnishes material for orchestral disportment representing the movements of an active ardor-filled crowd.

The chorus soon returns, however; forcibly chanting the happy hymn in its original simplicity, aided by the woodwinds repeating the chorus in following the melody, and often crossed by a diatonic design performed by all the strings in unison.

The following Andante maestoso is a kind of chorale first intoned by the tenors and basses of the chorus with trombones, 'cellos, and basses. The joy is religious, solemn, and immense.

The choir stops for an instant to resume its wide harmony more softly, after an orchestral solo producing an organ effect of great beauty. The imitation of the majestic instrument of Christian churches is produced by the lower register of the flute, the bass clarinet, the lower tones of the bassoon, the violas divided into high and medium parts, and the 'cellos playing on their open strings G, D, or C with its octave.

This movement starts in G, passes into C, and then into F, finishing by a pedal point on the dominant seventh of D. Succeeding it is a grand allegro in 6/4 where from the outset the first theme, already given in various ways, and the chorale of the foregoing andante, appear as one. The contrast of these two ideas is made even more striking by a rapid variation of the joyous song executed below the chorale's long notes by the first violins and the double basses.

It is impossible for double basses to execute so rapid a succession of notes,* and no one has been able to explain how a man as skillful in the

*According to all reports this was true even in Berlioz' time although the double-bass sections of the great symphonic orchestras of America and Europe give no evidence of this any more; and tackle the passage as if it were a standard exercise of relative simplicity — Ed.

art of instrumentation as Beethoven could possibly forget himself to the extent of writing a feature of this kind for this ponderous instrument.

In the next movement there is less manliness, less grandeur, and more lightness in style; in essence, it presents a simple gaiety, at first expressed by four solo voices, and later colored by the addition of the chorus. Twice in succession some tender and religious accents alternate with this gay melody, but the movement increases in its headlong fall. The entire orchestra breaks out; percussion instruments, including kettledrums, cymbals, triangle, and bass drum, firmly accent the strong beats of the bar. Joy returns triumphant, popular and tumultuous joy; almost resembling an orgy if all the voices, in terminating, did not pause again upon a solemn rhythm to project their last salute of love and respect to such joy by an ecstatic exclamation. The orchestra finishes alone before projecting fragments of the first theme, of which no one can tire, during its ardent course.

An exact as possible translation of the German poetry treated by Beethoven now gives the reader the key to this multitude of musical combinations, skilled auxiliaries of a genius both powerful and indefatigable.

Joy, source of light immortal, daughter of Elysium,
Touched with fire, to the portal of thy radiant shrine we come.
Thy pure magic frees all others held in custom's rigid rings;
*Men throughout the world are brothers in the haven of thy wings.**

This is the most difficult of all symphonies by this composer; its performance requiring patient and repeated study; but above all it must be well directed. Moreover, it requires a greater number of singers than would usually be needed because in many places the chorus is evidently supposed to cover the orchestra; and also because the way the music is set to words, and the excessive height of some of the vocal parts makes voice production difficult, and diminishes the volume and energy of the sounds produced.

Whatever may be said, Beethoven when finishing his work, and contemplating the majestic dimensions of the movement he had erected, certainly might very well have said to himself:

Now let death come, my task is done.

*Louis Untermeyer has provided a complete and new translation of Schiller's *Ode to Joy* adapted for use in performances of Beethoven's Ninth Symphony; in recorded broadcasts of The NBC Symphony Orchestra his translation was used by Arturo Toscanini who directed the orchestra, the chorus, and the soloists much as Berlioz did in London a century before. — Ed.

FIDELIO opera in three acts opus 72

the four overtures:
Leonore No. 2, C major, Opus 72a (1805)
Leonore No. 3, C major, Opus 72b (1806)
Leonore No. 1, C major, Opus 138 (1807)
Fidelio Overture, E major, Opus 72c (1814)

On the first of Ventose of the year VI (19 February 1798, according to the calendar of the French Revolution), the Rue Feydeau Theater produced *Leonora or Conjugal Love, historic fact, in two acts* (such was the title of this piece); words by M. Bouilly, music by P. Gaveaux. The work seemed only second rate despite the talent displayed by the actors of the principal parts: Gaveaux, the composer of the music, and Madame Scio, a great actress of that day.

A few years afterwards Paer wrote a graceful score to an Italian libretto where the Leonora of Bouilly was again the heroine; and it was coming away from a performance of this work that Beethoven, in his customary uncouth way, said to Paer: "I like your play. I have a good mind to set it to music."

This was the origin of the masterpiece we now consider. The first appearance of Beethoven's *Fidelio* on the German stage did not foretell its future celebrity; and it is reported performances were soon suspended. However, it reappeared sometime later, modified in several ways regarding the music and text; and it was given a new overture.

The second trial was a complete success. Beethoven, loudly recalled by the audience, was brought on stage after the first act, and again after the second act whose finale produced an enthusiasm heretofore unknown in Vienna. The score of *Fidelio,* however, was nevertheless the topic of varying degrees of bitter criticism. But from that moment it was performed on every stage in Germany; where ever since it has maintained its position; and where it now is part of the classical repertory.

London theaters extended it the same honor, somewhat later; and in 1827 it was welcomed with enthusiasm with a German troupe who gave it in Paris. The two main parts were sung with great talent by Haitzinger and Madame Schroeder-Devrient. It has just opened at the Theâtre-Lyrique in Paris; a fortnight ago it was on the stage of Covent Garden in London; and at the present moment they are playing it in New York. Tell me, if you can, at what theaters the *Leonora* of Gaveaux or of Paer is being performed? Only bookworms know of the existence of their operas. They are finished and no longer exist. Of the three scores the first is very weak; the second is hardly a work of talent; the third is a masterpiece of genius.

The more of Beethoven's work I hear, and the more of it I read, the more I find it worthy of admiration. The general effect, and its details, appear equally beautiful to me, for everywhere one finds energy, greatness, originality, and a mood as profound as it is true.

It belongs to that strong race of maligned works drenched in the most inconceivable prejudices, and the most manifest lies; but its vitality is so great nothing can prevail against it. They are like vigorous beeches, born amidst rocks and ruins, who end by splitting the rocks and piercing the rubble, and finally rising proud and verdant, all the more solidly implanted because of the obstacles they had to conquer in order to emerge; while willows growing without trouble along the river bank, fall into its bed, and die forgotten.

Beethoven wrote four overtures to his only opera. Having completed the first (*Leonore No. 2,* opus 72a) he began again, no one knowing exactly why, retaining the original arrangement and all the subjects, but joining them by different modulations, rescoring them, and adding a crescendo as well as a flute solo. In my opinion the solo is not up to the great style of the rest of the work. However, the composer seems to have preferred the second version (*Leonore No. 3,* opus 72b), as it was published first.

The manuscript of the original (*Leonore No. 2,* opus 72a) remained in the possession of Schindler, a friend of the composer, and was published only ten years ago by the firm of Richaut. I have had the honor of conducting it some twenty times at the Drury Lane Theatre in London, and at a few concerts in Paris; its effect is grand and exciting. The second version (*Leonore No. 3,* opus 72b), however, continues to retain the popularity it acquired under the name *Overture to Leonora,* and will probably keep it.

This superb overture, perhaps Beethoven's most beautiful, shared the fate of several sections of the opera, and was suppressed after the first performances. Another (also in C like the other two) charming and gentle in character, but with an ending not calculated to produce applause, met a similar fate (*Leonore No. 1,* opus 138) composed in 1807. Finally for the revival of his opera in modified form, the composer wrote an overture in E major (known as the *Fidelio Overture,* opus 72c); and it was adopted in preference to the other three. It is a masterful piece containing incomparable life and light, a real symphonic masterpiece, but it does not fit the opera it introduces either in character or material. The other overtures are, to some extent, the opera of *Fidelio* abridged, presenting along with the tender accents of Leonora, the sorrowful plaint of the prisoner dying of hunger, the delightful trio melodies of the final act, the distant trumpet fanfare announcing the arrival of Don Fernando, the minister of justice who will free Florestan; in fact they throb with dramatic interest, and are real overtures in *Fidelio.*

The principal theaters of Germany and England, realizing after thirty or forty years that the second Leonore overture (*Leonore No. 3,* the first published) was a magnificent work, perform it now as an entracte between the first and second acts, keeping the overture in E major (the *Fidelio Overture,* opus 72c) for the actual opening. It is a pity the Theâtre-Lyrique has not seen fit to follow their example. We should even like to see the Conservatoire do the same as Mendelssohn did at a Gewandhaus concert in Leipzig, and give us at one of its performances the whole of the four overtures to Beethoven's opera. But this would most likely seem to be an experiment too bold for Paris; and boldness, as we know, is not a defect of our musical institutions.

The subject matter of *Fidelio,* for something must be said about the piece itself, is sad and melodramatic; and has contributed greatly to feed the prejudice of the French public against the opera. The story concerns a political prisoner whom the prison governor wishes to starve in his dungeon. The prisoner's wife, Leonore, disguised as a young boy under the name Fidelio, ingratiates herself as a servant with Rocco, the jailer.

Marzelline, Rocco's daughter, is engaged to the turnkey Jaquino, but being seduced by Fidelio's enticing appearance, she soon neglects her rustic suitor in favor of this newcomer.

Don Pizarro, the governor of the prison, impatient for the death of his victim, and not finding hunger swift enough, resolves to go and strangle him where he lies. Rocco is ordered to dig a hole in the corner of the dungeon where the prisoner's corpse is to be thrown.

Rocco selects Fidelio to aid him in this ghastly task; and the poor woman is in anguish to find herself so near her husband, who is about to succumb, but whom she dare not approach. Soon cruel Don Pizarro appears; the shackled prisoner rises, recognizes his executioner, and challenges him; Pizarro advances with a dagger in his hand just as Fidelio thrusting herself between them, draws a pistol from her bosom, and points it at the face of Don Pizarro who retreats in fright.

At this moment a trumpet is heard from afar. It is the distant signal to lower the drawbridge and raise the prison gate. The arrival of the minister of justice is announced. The prison governor is prevented from

51

finishing his bloodthirsty deed; he rushes from the dungeon, and the prisoner is saved.

When the minister of justice appears he recognizes Pizarro's victim as his friend Florestan. Happiness is widespread except for the confusion of poor Marzelline, who upon learning Fidelio is a woman, is obliged to return to her Jaquino.

At the Théâtre-Lyrique they have thought it advisable to trace an altogether new drama over this work of Bouilly. The scene of the latter is laid in Milan during 1495; its principal characters are Ludovic Sforza, his wife, Jean Galleas, Isabella of Aragon, and Charles VIII, King of France. Thus they are able to conclude with a brilliant tableau; one set off with costumes less somber than those of the original piece.

Such was the only reason, poor as it was, for inducing M. Carvalho, the able director of this playhouse, when *Fidelio* was being rehearsed, to want such a substitution. They do not admit in France a foreign opera should be translated purely and simply. Nevertheless the work was performed without much prejudice to its score; as all the characters remained united to situations of a sort similar to those originally written.

As far as the Parisian public is concerned, what stands in the way of the music of *Fidelio,* is the chasteness of its melody, the composer's great disdain for unjustified sonorous effects, and his contempt for conventional endings and phrases. The opulent sobriety of his orchestration is another cause, as well as the boldness of his harmony, and beyond all, I will venture to say, the depth of his feeling for expression. Everything must be heard in his complex music, everything must be listened to, to enable us to understand it.

The orchestral parts, sometimes principal and sometimes obscure, may contain the exact accent of expression, the cry of passion, the very idea the composer may not have been able to give the vocal part. This does not suggest any lack of the latter's predominance as those pretend, who never tire of harping on the old reproaches. One addressed by Grétry to Mozart ran: *He put the pedestal on the stage and the statue in the orchestra.* But the same criticism had already been addressed to Gluck, and was later applied to Weber, Spontini, and Beethoven. It will never cease to be addressed to any composer who abstains from penning platitudes for the voice; and who gives the orchestra an interesting part, however much learning and discretion he may display.

The people who are so quick to blame the great masters for a pretended predominance of instruments over voices do not greatly esteem this learning or this discretion. Every day for the last ten years we have seen the orchestra turned into a military band, a blacksmith's forge, or a brazier's shop, without this alarming the critics, and ever causing them to pay the slightest attention to these enormities. The critics say nothing if the orchestra is noisy, violent, brutal, insipid, revolting, and even exterminating the voice and the melody. But it is fine and intelligent if it attracts a certain attention to itself by its vivacity, grace, and eloquence and, if in spite of all this it still plays the part assigned by dramatic and musical exigence, it is blamed. The orchestra is easily pardoned either for saying nothing at all or for uttering nothing but stupidity and coarseness in the event it should speak.

Without counting the four overtures there are sixteen numbers in the score of *Fidelio*. There were more in the original. Some were suppressed at the time of the second production of the opera in Vienna, as well as many cuts and modifications made at the same time in the remaining numbers.

It was in 1855, I think, when a Leipzig editor decided to publish the complete original work, indicating the cuts and changes inflicted. The study of this curious score furnishes an idea of the tortures the impatient Beethoven was called upon to suffer in having to submit to these revisions. This he did no doubt in a spirit of rage, comparing himself to the slave of Alfieri.

In Germany, as in Italy, as in France, as everywhere in the theater, everyone, without exception, knows better than the composer. The latter is a public enemy and, if a printer's devil or other apprentice thinks such and such a piece of music by any master is too long, everyone will consider him right against either Gluck, Weber, Mozart, Rossini, or Beethoven. Regarding Rossini, see the insolent suppressions made in his *William Tell* both before and after the first appearance of that work of art. The theater, for both poets and musicians, is a school of humility; for poets there get lessons from those who know naught of grammar while musicians are taken in hand by those who know nothing of the scale; and every captious critic, prejudiced against anything appearing to be new or daring, is full of an unconquerable love for the prudent and for the commonplace.

All sixteen numbers of Beethoven's *Fidelio* have a beautiful and noble visage. But they are beautiful in different ways, and that is precisely what seems to me to be their main merit. The first duet, between Marzelline and her lover, is set apart from the others by its style. This is familiar, gay, and of piquant simplicity, so the character of the two individuals is revealed at once. The aria in C minor of the young girl seems in melodic form to approach the style of Mozart's best examples. The orchestra, however, is treated with a care more minute than ever exercised by the illustrious predecessor of Beethoven.

An exquisitely melodious quartet follows; and is treated as a canon in the octave; each of the voices entering in turn to announce the theme in such a way as to produce a solo accompanied by a small orchestra of cellos, violas, and clarinets; and then a duet, plus a trio, and a complete quartet.

Rossini wrote many ravishing things in the same form, such as the canon in *Moses: Mi manca la voce*. But the canon in *Fidelio* is an andante, not succeeded by the usual allegro with cabalette and noisy coda; so the public, although charmed by its graceful movement, remains surprised, and is not able to understand why the allegro finale with its cadence, its whip crack, does not arrive. (By the way — why not give it some whip cracks?)

Rocco's couplets regarding the power of gold, as written by Gaveaux in the French score, may now be compared to those in Beethoven's German score. Of all the numbers in Gaveaux' opera this is probably the best one to use in making such a comparison. Beethoven's melody has a jovial charm whose vigorous simplicity is varied midway by a modulation and a time change. Gaveaux', although less lofty in style, has no less interest due to its melodic frankness as well as the excellent diction and its tasteful orchestration.

Beethoven begins to use a more spacious form in the following trio; a vast development and a richer and more agitated orchestration. We feel we are now entering upon the real drama whose coming passion is revealed by distant lightning.

A march appears with extremely attractive melody and modulation although its general color seems sad as might be expected in a march of soldiers guarding a prison. The first two notes of the theme, struck softly by the kettledrums, with brasses pizzicato, contribute to make it even more somber. Neither this march nor the preceding trio have any counterpart in the opera of Gaveaux, and the same may be said of many other numbers in Beethoven's rich score.

Among these is Pizarro's aria, and although it receives no applause in Paris, we ask permission to treat it as a masterpiece. In this terrible number the ferocious joy of a monster about to satisfy his vengeance is depicted with the most awful truth. Beethoven in his opera has carefully observed Gluck's precept not to use instruments except in relation to the degree of interest and passion required. Here, for the first time, the entire orchestra is released, starting with an uproar on the chord of the minor ninth of D minor. Everything trembles and is agitated; cries and blows abound; the vocal part, it is true, is a mere declamation. And what savage intensity its accent acquires when, having established the major mode, the composer makes the guard's chorus intervene; their voices, first murmuring an accompaniment to Pizarro's, at last breaks out at the end with force. It is admirable. I have heard this sung in Germany, in overpowering fashion, by Pischek.

The duet for two basses between Rocco and the governor is not quite up to this level but still I cannot approve of the liberty they took at the Théâtre-Lyrique in suppressing it.

A similar liberty, although one taken with the more or less real consent of the composer, was the case of the charming duet for sopranos, sung by Fidelio and Marzelline, where one violin and one 'cello, aided by a few orchestral entries, accompany the two voices with such elegance. This duet, found in the Leipzig score mentioned, has been reinstalled in Beethoven's work at the Théâtre-Lyrique. The wise guys of the Paris theater do not agree with those of Vienna. How lucky there should be a difference of opinion between them. Except for that we should have been prevented from ever hearing this musical dialogue — so fresh, so sweet, so elegant.

They say we owe this reinstallation to the prompter of the Theâtre-Lyrique. Bravo, prompter!

The great aria of *Fidelio* is with recitative, adagio cantabile and allegro finale, accompanied by three horns and one bassoon obbligati. I find the recitative a fine dramatic moment; the adagio made sublime by its tender accents and melancholy graces; the allegro made exciting, being full of noble enthusiasm and magnificence, even to the degree of being well worthy of serving as the model for Agatha's aria in *Der Freischütz*. I know excellent critics are not of my opinion; but I am quite content not to be of theirs.

The allegro theme of this admirable aria is introduced by three horns and solo bassoon, confining themselves to sounding five notes: B, E, G, B, E, occupying five bars of incredible originality. You might give these five notes to any musician who does not know them, and I wager in a hundred combinations there will be not one to equal the proud and impetuous phrase Beethoven draws from them, as the rhythm used is entirely unforeseen. This allegro strikes many as having one great fault: it does not have any little phrase they can remember easily. These amateurs, insensible to the many and striking beauties of this number, just look out for their four-bar phrases like children looking for a prize in a Christmas cake, or like country people looking for a high B whenever a new tenor appears.

The cake might be exquisite, and the tenor the most delightful singer in the world, but neither one nor the other would have any success: *There's no prize inside that cake! Where's his high note?* Agatha's aria in *Der Freischütz* is almost popular; but then it has the note. How many pieces, even by Rossini, that prince of melodists, have remained in the shade because they lacked the note.

The tone of the horns, somewhat veiled and even painful, blends perfectly with the mournful joy and uneasy hope filling the heart of Leonora. It is as sweet and tender as the cooing of doves. Spontini, without ever having heard Beethoven's *Fidelio,* used the horns with a very similar intention in accompanying *Toi que j'implore* in *La Vestale.* Several masters since then, Donizetti among them, paid Beethoven the same compliment in *Lucia.*

The emotion produced by the prisoners' chorus, no less poignant, is equally profound. A troop of unfortunates leave their dungeons then and come for a moment to breathe the air in the prison square. As they enter, listen to those first few bars of the orchestra, to those sweet and broad harmonies seeming to open out so radiantly; and to those timid voices grouping slowly but at last arriving at a harmonic expansion apparently exhaled by those breasts habitually oppressed; exactly like a sigh of happiness. And to the melodious design accompanying them. Again one might ask: why did the composer not give the melodic design to the voices and the vocal parts to the orchestra?

Why? Because it would have been evident clumsiness. The voices sing exactly as they ought to sing. One note more placed in the vocal parts would spoil the correctness and the truth of an expression so profoundly felt. The instrumental design is only a secondary idea, however melodious it may be, and it well suits the woodwinds and brings out the sweetness of the vocal harmonies, so ingeniously placed above the orchestra, to perfection. No composer of good sense could, I believe, be found (no matter to what school he might belong) to disapprove of Beethoven's idea in this instance.

The prisoners' happiness is disturbed momentarily by the appearance of the guards charged with watching them. The musical color changes immediately; all becomes gloomy and dull. But the guards have finished their round; their suspicious glances have ceased to weigh upon their captives. Accordingly the tonality of the episodic passage of the chorus gradually approaches that of the principal key. Closer and closer it comes; the key is touched; and then there is a short silence. And now the first theme reappears in the primitive key so true to nature I will not try to even give an idea of it as it is the light, the air, sweet liberty and life given back to us.

Some listeners, drying their eyes at the end of this chorus, are indignant about the silence, feeling the place should again echo with immense applause. It is possible most of the public is really moved; but there are certain kinds of beauty, apparent to all, and yet not calculated to excite applause.

The prisoners' chorus in Gaveaux' opera: *Que ce beau ciel, cette verdure,* etc., is written about the same theme but, alas, compared with that of Beethoven it seems very gloomy and flat. Let us also remark that the French composer, who is very careful about using his trombones in the remainder of his score, lets them enter here, exactly as if they belonged to the family of instruments possessed of a timbre sweet, calm, and suave. Whoever can explain this strange fancy?

In the second part of the duet, where Rocco tells Fidelio they are going to dig the prisoner's grave, there is a syncopated design for woodwinds; its effect is very strange, but its sighing rhythm and uneasy movement adapt it perfectly to this situation. The duet and the following quintet contain some very fine passages. A few approach, as far as style is concerned, Mozart's manner in *The Marriage of Figaro.*

A quintet with chorus ends this act. In this piece, whose color is correctly somber, a somewhat dry modulation appears brusquely about halfway through; and some of the voices execute rhythms barely distinguishable from others, but without its ever appearing just what the composer had in mind. The mystery, however, reigning over the ensemble, gives the finale a most dramatic aspect; and it finishes *piano,* expressive of dismay and fear. So the Parisian public does not applaud; being unable to applaud an ending so contrary to its usual habits.

Before the curtain rises for the third act the orchestra plays a slow and lugubrious symphony filled with long cries of anguish, sobs, tremblings, and heavy pulsations. We are about to enter a scene of pain and grief; Florestan is stretched upon his bed of straw; and we are to witness his agony and hear his delirious cries.

Gluck's orchestration for the dungeon scene of Orestes in *Iphigenia in Taurus* is no doubt very beautiful; but to what heights does Beethoven soar above his rival. Not just because he is a great symphonist, or because he better knows how to make the orchestra speak; but — it is important to remember — his musical thought in this number is stronger, grander, and infinitely more penetrating. We feel from the very first bars that the unfortunate occupant of the dungeon must, on entering it, have left all hope behind.

The description follows. A mournful recitative, interspersed by the principal phrases of the preceding symphony, is followed by a desolate and heartrending cantabile whose sadness is constantly increased by the accompaniment of the woodwinds. The prisoner's grief becomes more and more intense. His brain wanders as he has been touched by the wing of death. Overcome by a sudden hallucination he imagines himself free; he smiles as tears of tenderness roll out of his dying eyes. He imagines he sees his wife again; and that he calls and she answers. He is intoxicated with the idea of liberty and love.

To others must fall the task of depicting this melody of sobs; these palpitations of the orchestra; the faithful song of the oboe following that of Florestan like the voice of the adored wife he thinks he hears; that exciting crescendo, and the last cry of the dying man. I cannot do it.

Now let us recognize the sovereign art, the burning inspiration, and the electric flight of genius.

Florestan has fallen back upon his pallet after this feverish fit; Rocco now appears, accompanied by the trembling Leonora (Fidelio).

The terror of this scene diminishes in the new libretto making it a mere question of cleaning out a cistern instead of digging the grave of a prisoner who is still alive. (This shows you what *improvements* lead to.)

Nothing could be more sinister than this celebrated duet where the cold insensibility of Rocco is contrasted with the heartrending asides of Fidelio; and where the dull murmur of the orchestra might be likened to the dead sound of earthen clods falling on a coffin. One of our critics has very correctly referred to a resemblance between this number and the gravediggers' scene in Hamlet. He could not have given it any greater or higher praise.

The gravediggers of Beethoven finish their duet without any coda. They also have no cabalette and no vocal demonstration of any kind.

Therefore the pit preserves a rigorous silence. You see where the trouble is!

The pistol quartet is one long roll of thunder whose threatening mood increases continually and concludes in a series of explosions. After the cry of Fidelio: "I am his wife," the musical and dramatic forces are no longer distinguishable. The listener is moved, excited, or disturbed without being able to decide if his emotion is due to the voices, the instruments, or the dramatic action.

The voices, challenging each other and answering in heated apostrophes, are always heard above the tumult of the orchestra; and across this we hear the strings sounding like the clamoring of a crowd agitated by a thousand passions. It is a miracle of dramatic music without counterpart I know of in any master, either ancient or modern.

The alteration of the libretto has inflicted enormous injury upon this beautiful scene. As the action had been transferred to a time when the pistol had not yet been invented, they were obliged to forego giving it to Fidelio as an offensive weapon. The younger woman, therefore, threatens Pizarro with an iron bar. This is incomparably less dangerous, and especially for such a man, than the little tube with which a weak hand could have struck him dead by making the slightest movement. The very gesture of Fidelio taking aim at Pizarro's face imparts a grand scenic effect. I can still see Madame Devrient stretching out her trembling arm in Pizarro's direction, and laughing with a convulsive laugh.

After this admirable quartet the couple, being left alone, sing a duet of equal excellence where intense passion, joy, surprise, and depression borrow in turn from the music an expression it would be impossible to convey to anyone who has not heard it. What love, what transports, what fervor! With what passion they embrace! How they stammer out of sheer earnestness! The words crowd to their trembling lips; they stagger, they are breathless, in short they love!

What is in common between such transports of affection and the insipid duets of those united by a mere conventional marriage?

In the final finale we have an extensive concerted number whose march rhythm is first interrupted by a few episodic slow movements. The allegro is then resumed and proceeds with increasing animation and sonority to the very end. In this peroration the coldest and most stubborn listeners are dazzled and captivated by its majesty, and by its extraordinary life. Then they put on an air of gracious approval, saying: *"Not so bad."*

But then all the remainder of the score, although it moves them so little, is nevertheless admirable for that, and without wishing to downgrade this gigantic finale, several of the preceding numbers are not only superior but even much superior.

Yet who knows if light may not come sooner than we expect even to those whose hearts are now closed to this fine work of Beethoven, as they are also now closed to the Ninth Symphony, the last quartets, and the great piano sonatas of this incomparable master?

Sometimes a thick veil seems to be placed before the mind's eye as it glances towards one region of the heavenly expanse of art. It is thereby prevented from seeing the great planets illumining this portion. But all at once, for some unknown cause, the veil is torn away. Then at last we see; and blush at having been blind so long.

This reminds me of poor Adolphe Nourrit. One day he said to me that in all of Shakespeare's work he found only *Macbeth* admirable; and he regarded *Hamlet* as unintelligible and absurd. Three years later he came to me saying: "*Hamlet* is the greatest philosophic poet who ever lived. Now I understand it. My heart and my head are filled with it. It intoxicates me. You must have a singular opinion of my poetic sense and intelligence. Give me back your esteem."

Alas, poor Yorick!

Musical Terminology

adagio — slow; slow movement of a symphony

allegretto — cheerful; symphonic movement slower than allegro

allegro — very fast; fast movement of a symphony

andante — moderately slow; symphonic movement slower than allegro

appogiatura — grace note

arco — bow

aria — song for solo voice often accompanied by an orchestra or some instrument such as the piano

assai — very; very much

basses — lowest-voiced male singers; lowest-voiced string instruments

brasses — brass instruments such as french horns, trumpets, trombones

cabalette — song sung with variations including accompaniment in triplets suggesting hoof beats (derived from *cabaletta* — Italian for little horse)

canon — musical question and answer or statement and response

cantabile — lyric; lyrical

cello — violoncello

col arco — resume bowing; musical direction given after strings have been playing pizzicato

con brio — with fire; with spirit; with vigor; with vivacity

con moto — with motion; with speed

Conservatoire — conservatory; school of music; usually when capitalized the Conservatory of Paris or its orchestra

coryphée — leader of a section of a ballet or chorus

crescendo — increasing in volume

diminuendo — diminishing in volume

double basses — lowest-voiced string instruments

duet — composition for two instruments or two singers

entracte — music played between the acts

finale — conclusion; last movement of a symphony

forte — loud

fugato — freely; in the manner of a fugue

Gewandhaus — ancient market hall of Leipzig famous for its concerts, especially those performed by the orchestra of the Leipzig Conservatory founded by Mendelssohn

grupetto — a small group; a small trill

horns — french horns

idyll — a pastoral

larghetto — slow but not quite as slow as largo; slow movement of a symphony

maestoso — majestic(ally)

marcia funebre — funeral march

martellato — hammering; strongly struck notes as in kettledrumming performed with hard-headed sticks

menuetto — minuet; formal dancelike movement of a symphony

mezzoforte — moderately loud

molto — extremely; much; very much

non — no; not

non troppo — not too much

obbligato — indispensable accompaniment

organ point — pedal point where one tone is sustained in a phrase by independent harmonies

ostinato — continuous; obstinate as in the obstinate bowing of the basses
Paris Conservatoire — see Conservatoire
pedal — see organ point
percussion — instruments played by striking as in bass drums, cymbals, kettledrums, pianos, triangles, et cetera
pianissimo — extremely soft; very soft
piano — soft; softly
piano — keyboard percussion instrument
pizzicato — plucked as in string instruments played by plucking as an alternate to bowing
poco — a little; somewhat
presto — fast; symphonic movement played in rapid time
punta d'arco — played with the point or tip of the bow
recitative — musical declamation or recitation
ritornello — repeated portion or refrain
scherzando — gay, mirthful, sportive
scherzo — fun-filled musical movement developed by Beethoven from the minuet, and often the second or third movement of a symphony dating from his time
sostenuto — sustained
strings — stringed instruments such as violins, violas, cellos, double basses
tempo — speed; time
tremolo — quivering trill; trembling trill
tutti — all the orchestra; all the strings; et cetera
un — a; an; one
un poco — a little
vivace — briskly; lively; faster than allegro; quickly; with vivacity
winds — woodwinds
woodwinds — bassoons, clarinets, flutes, oboes, piccolos; instruments whose tone is produced by breathing over an opening as in a flute or piccolo or through a reed or reeds as is the case with bassoons, oboes, and clarinets; at one time all these were made of wood although most of this is now replaced by metals and plastics

RALPH DE SOLA, an ardent concert-goer and music lover, grew up surrounded by composers, musicians, and concert artists. His lifelong interest in music led him to compile and translate Berlioz' essays in the present book. He is the author of fourteen books on subjects as diverse as abbreviations, cooking, martime history, microfilming, and wildlife, and he frequently reviews classical music concerts and recordings.

Mr. De Sola teaches English at Mesa College (San Diego), and was Publications Editor at Convair for more than fourteen years.

Some of the best critical commentary on Ludwig van Beethoven's music came from the pen of composer Hector Berlioz over a hundred years ago. The essays in this book are translated from Berlioz' original collection, *A travers chants,* published in 1862. They deal perceptively with the musical content and impact of Beethoven's nine symphonies and his only opera, *Fidelio,* and its four overtures, and are as fresh and meaningful today as when they were written.

Here are insights into the music of one of the world's greatest composers by a fellow artist separated from his subject by only a few years; Berlioz was an early conductor of Beethoven's works, and he was in a unique position to understand his music.

Modern listeners and students now have the opportunity to share his knowledge and add to their enjoyment and understanding of Beethoven's nine symphonies and *Fidelio* in this excellent new translation.

Included are brief chronologies of the lives of both composers and musical terminology.

593